Doc Jim's
Book of
WHO CARES!?
Trivia you never wanted to know, but may need someday!

James Charles Bouffard, Psy.D., Ph.D.

(Edited by: Lisa Diane Branscome)

Illustrated

Lynn Paulo Foundation
Pomona, California

ISBN 978-0-557-02028-7

Printed in the United States of America

Other works by Dr. Bouffard:

Be A Private Investigator
The Magician's Fight!
A Quest For Absolute Power
The Entrepreneurial Ben Franklin
DEFIANCE! A Saga of David Crockett and the Alamo

Dedicated to:
Lisa Diane Branscome
Even while editing this work,
she was heard to mumble,
"Who cares!?"

Acknowledgments

The author gratefully acknowledges Thomas Gale's Nineteenth Century U.S. Newspaper database, University of Arizona/Department of Journalism, University Library of Heidelberg, Charles F. Home's *Great Men and Famous women*, University of North Carolina at Chapel Hill, Victoria and Albert Museum [London], Cedar Rapids Museum [Grand Rapids, MI], National Postal Museum, National Institutes of Health, University of Houston, U.S. National Oceanic and Atmospheric Administration, Niagara Falls Public Library, Los Angeles Police Department, R.C.M.P.[Royal Canadian Mounted Police] Archives, *The Book of Knowledge* [The Grolier Society, 1911] The Grolier Club, National Archives and Records Administration, Musée des arts at métiers — France, NASA Headquarters, National Museum of American History, U. S. Department of Treasury and the Library of Congress for needed information and their kind permission to reproduce illustrations within this work.

Forward

Throughout the centuries, intelligent men and women have quested for diverse information. Whether this acquired knowledge was important or not, they bracketed it away for some future use.

Eventually the notable data surfaced, while its less significant facts remained profoundly buried within that portion of the brain that mouthed "Who cares!?" to each frivolous piece discovered.

In 1884, Mark Twain humorously prefaced his disdain for trivia in *The Adventures of Huckleberry Finn*: "Persons attempting to find a motive in this narrative will be prosecuted; persons attempting to find a moral in it will be banished; persons attempting to find a plot in it will be shot."

When Twain sat to write this sequel to *The Adventures of Tom Sawyer*, he seriously doubted his ability to continue the moralistic lessons garnered from what he considered a store of useless knowledge.

Huckleberry Finn's preface waxed ironic over time, however, since this novel definitely had a motive, was demurely moralistic, and gave us an unforgettable plot; far surpassing *Tom Sawyer*'s light-hearted, if enjoyable, escapades and hijinks.

First recorded to have originated in England around 1589, trivia (or trivium) referred to insignificant facts considered of interest solely to undergraduate students of the Liberal Arts.

Gradually, the term modified to represent any information of little importance to the general public.

By the 20th century a unique form of communication was to lay open a way for trivia to re-emerge in a different light. In 1935 *Professor Dick and His Question Box*, hosted by British/Canadian Roy Ward Dickson (1910 –1978), was the first of many radio quiz shows.

Then, in 1940 and 1950, Ralph Edwards (1913 – 2005) introduced radio and television audiences, respectively, to *Truth or Consequences*.

As the first televised quiz show, Edwards and the growing popularity of this new media brought excitement and money to contestants who felt blessed with their garnered bits of intelligence, although many soon preferred to answer the trivia questions incorrectly in order to perform the zany and embarrassing stunts of the "Consequences" portion of the show.

Moving over the years, Dell Publishing Company produced the first *Trivia* book in 1966, which would soon land a spot on the New York Times Best Sellers list. From 1974 to 1981 the success of such volumes as ***The Trivia Encyclopedia***, ***The Complete Unabridged Super Trivia Encyclopedia*** and ***Super Trivia, vol. II*** led to further trivial pursuits.

On September 4, 1998, the United Kingdom ushered in ***Who Wants to Be a Millionaire*** (original working title: ***Cash Mountain***), spreading the trivia phenomena over more than fifty countries, culminating to a brain awakening success in the United States.

No one was saying "Who cares!?" to trivia anymore. Not if they wanted to appear smarter than their neighbors.

This work is not a modest collection of trivial data filched from an Internet search, since information of this type is not altogether accurate. Nor does it lean on circumstances thought true for years, yet found unreliable under tight examination.

Rather, the author has thoroughly researched each piece of trivia enclosed within these pages, sourcing many with dates, records, photos and period artwork for the most accurate of obtainable facts.

So sit back, dear reader, and open your mind to a world you may have once dismissed with an utterance of "Who cares!?"

But then, irrespective of how you should feel after reading this little volume, wouldn't it be nice to take home a lot of extra money because you knew something someone else didn't?

Doc Jim
August 16, 2008

"Why is it trivia? People call it trivia because they know nothing and they are embarrassed about it."
Robbie Coltrane
Scottish actor, comedian, author
(Rubeus Hagrid, *Harry Potter* movies)

Contents

"Time spent staring into space while thinking is not time wasted."

Willis Haviland Carrier

(1876 – 1950)

Inventor of the modern air conditioner.

Illustrations List

Illustrations List

Doc Jim's
Book of
WHO CARES

American Trivia

Did You Know:

The names of the two lions sitting in front of the New York Public Library, Fifth Avenue at 42nd Street, New York City, are Patience and Fortitude.

Borden County, Texas is named for Gail Borden (1801 – 1874), the man who drew the first topographical map of Texas, surveyed and plotted the city of Galveston, and introduced us to condensed milk.

The average American earned $100 a week until 1963.

Rhode Island takes in the least amount of annual tourist dollars, while California takes in the most.

The only United States city below sea level, not in the California desert, is New Orleans, Louisiana.

There are 1,860 steps to the top of New York City's Empire State Building. [From street level to the 102nd floor.]

Civilian Neil Armstrong was the first astronaut launched into space by the United States [1966].

Charles Joseph Bonaparte (1851 – 1921), grandnephew of France's Napoléon I (1769 – 1821), formed the Federal Bureau of Investigation [F.B.I] on July 26, 1908.

He was then the United States Attorney General [1906-09] under President Theodore Roosevelt [1901-09].

The public rest rooms, at five 5¢ a visit, earned $862.00 in five months at the Chicago World's Fair of 1933-34 [Century of Progress].

The White House, then known as the President's Mansion, accepted John Adam's (1735 – 1826) as her first occupant in 1800.

Eighty-seven year old Rebecca Latimer Felton (1835 – 1930) became the first woman U.S. Senator when she was appointed to serve the remaining day of a vacated Georgia senate seat [November 21-22, 1922]. And, as of this writing, is the only woman to serve as a Georgia Senator.

Rebecca Latimer Felton
(1835 – 1930)
First woman U.S. Senator.
Photo courtesy: National Photo Company
Collection, Library of Congress

Diplomat Ralph Bunche (1903 – 1971) was the first African-American to win the Nobel Peace Prize ["...mediation of the 1948 –49 Arab-Israeli War."] in 1950.

Senator Henry Clay's (1777 – 1852) body was the first to lie in state in the Rotunda of the Capital Building, Washington, DC [1852].

Henry Clay, Sr.
(1777 – 1852)
First person to lie in state in the
Rotunda of the United States
Capital, Washington, DC.
Daguerreotype courtesy: Library of Congress
[Photographer: Mathew Brady, 1822 – 1896]

Washington's Jefferson Memorial, due to its domed ceiling, has often been criticized as looking like a muffin.

President Calvin Coolidge (1872 – 1933) declared New York Harbor's Statue of Liberty a National Monument on October 15, 1924.

The first United States citizen canonized by the Roman Catholic Church was Frances Xavier Cabrini [known as Mother Cabrini] (1850 – 1917) on July 17, 1946 by Pope Pius XII (1876 – 1958).

Mother Cabrini
(1850 – 1917)
First canonized citizen
of the United States.
Photo courtesy: Library of Congress

The flag of the United States is folded into a triangle to represent the tricorn hats worn by Revolutionary War soldiers.

Delaware is known as "The First State" because it was the first to ratify the United States Constitution [December 7, 1787].

Annie Moore (1877 – 1923) was the first immigrant to pass through Ellis Island for entrance into the United States [1892]. She was then a 15-year-old from County Cork, Ireland.

As an initial process to the newly opened facility, she was presented with a ten dollar gold piece.

Her brothers [Philip and Anthony] followed her through the line, where all three were met by the press.

She would move in with her parents, who had come to the United States in 1888 and were living at 32 Monroe St., Manhattan, marry a few years later, have eleven children, and spend the rest of her life working toward her American dream in New York.

Artist's contemporary illustration of 15-year-old Annie Moore as she entered the United States through Ellis Island, New York Harbor on her birthday, January 1, 1892.
Courtesy: Thomas Gale's *Nineteenth Century U.S. Newspaper* database

Charles Carroll (1737 – 1832) of Carrollton, Maryland was the last surviving signer of the Declaration of Independence.

Pamphleteer Thomas Paine (1737 – 1809) was the first to coin our nation *United States of America* [January 13, 1777].

The thirteen stars on the first United States flag [1777] were sewn into a circle so no one colony could view itself above the other.

Josh Bean (1818 – 1852), older brother of Judge Roy Bean (1825 – 1903) [Law West of the Pecos], was the first United States mayor of San Diego, California [1850].

On August 5, 1861, President Abraham Lincoln [1861-65] signed the Revenue Act, imposing the first Federal Income Tax

Although Lincoln's tax law was repealed in 1871, the 16th Amendment, passed in 1909 and later ratified in 1913, set in place today's Federal Income Tax system.

Juneau, Alaska was named for Canadian Joseph Juneau (1836 – 1903), the prospector who discovered gold in the Alaskan panhandle in 1880.

Joseph Juneau
(1836 – 1899)
Alaska's capital city is
named for this prospect-
or and co-founder.
Photo courtesy: Library of Congress

It took two hundred and fourteen crates to transport the Statue of Liberty from France to New York in 1885.

The Pledge of Allegiance was written by Francis Julius Bellamy (1855 – 1931) to commemorate the 400th anniversary of Columbus' discovery of America. [Published on September 8, 1892 in the *Youth's Companion* magazine.]

The Gunfight at the O.K. Corral between the Earps and "the cow-boys" actually took place in vacant lot #2, block 17, behind the corral. With some of the fighting spreading into Fremont Street, bordering the vacant lot.

The time and date of the conflict has been recorded as "about 3:00 p.m., Wednesday, October 26, 1881."

ARIZONA.

A Desperate Fight Between Officers of the Law and Cow-boys — The Killed and Wounded — Failure of Lord & Williams.

TOMBSTONE, A. T., October 26th. — This morning the City Marshal, V. W. Earp, arrested a cow-boy named Ike Clanton, for disorderly conduct, and he was fined twenty-five dollars and disarmed in the Justices' Court. Clanton left, swearing vengeance on the Sheriff and Marshal Earp and his brother Morgan who tried to induce Clanton to leave the town, but he refused to be pacified. About three o'clock P. M., the Earp brothers and J. H. Halliday met four cow-boys, namely, the two Clanton brothers and the two McLowery brothers, when a lively fire commenced from the cow-boys against the three citizens. About thirty shots were fired rapidly. When the smoke of battle

***The Tombstone Epitaph*'s recounting of the Gunfight of the O.K. Corral [1881].**
Courtesy:
The Tombstone Epitaph
University of Arizona/ Department of Journalism
Marshall Building, Room 334
645 N. Park Ave.
Tucson, AZ 85721-0158

Calamity Jane [Martha Jane Cannary, 1856 – 1903) was buried next to gunfighter, gambler and lawman "Wild Bill" James Butler Hickok (1837 – 1876) in Deadwood, South Dakota, wearing a white dress and holding a gun in each hand.

Calamity Jane, age 43
(1856 – 1903)
Photo courtesy: Library of Congress
[Photographer: Henry R. Locke, 1895]

The first execution by lethal gas in American history was carried out in Carson City, Nevada on February 8, 1924.

Tong Lee, member of a Chinese gang convicted of murdering a rival gang member, was the man executed.

Due to the segregation laws of 1941, Dr. Charles Richard Drew (1904 – 1950), who had organized the first blood bank in the United States, was unable to donate his own blood. He was black.

The two dollar bill, with the portrait of Thomas Jefferson on its face, was officially discontinued as a United States Note in 1966.

It was re-assigned as a Federal Reserve Note in 1976 to commemorate the United States Bicentennial, but is in rare use today.

Series 1953 two dollar bill, discontinued as a United States Note in 1966.

Courtesy:
United States Department of Treasury
1500 Pennsylvania Ave. NW
Washington, DC 20220
[Note: Fraudulent enlargement and/or use of this image is punishable under present counterfeiting laws.]

"My reading is extremely eclectic. Lately I've been teaching myself computer graphics, so I'm learning a lot about that. I read books of trivia, of facts."
Jack Prelutsky
poet and author

Art & Book Trivia

Did You Know:

While studying at the Academy of Ancient Art in the Medici Palace, Michelangelo (1475 – 1564) was struck in the face with a mallet wielded by rival Pietro Torregiano (1472 – ca 1522), crushing his nose and disfiguring him for life.

A Study in Scarlet was the first published Sherlock Holmes story, written by 27-year-old Arthur Conan Doyle (1859 – 1930) in 1887 for £ 25.

Edgar Rice Burroughs (1875 – 1950), creator of *Tarzan*,

was the first author to incorporate himself [1923].

Cyrano de Bergerac (1619 – 1655) wrote of fantastic excursions to both the moon and the sun two hundred years before Jules Verne (1828 – 1905).

Cyrano de Bergerac
(1619 – 1655)
French satirist, dramatist and legendary duelist
Image in author's collection

Edgar Allen Poe (1809 – 1849) was expelled from West Point for appearing in a public parade [for a very short period] wearing nothing more than a white belt and gloves.

Harriet Beecher Stowe's (1811 – 1896) *Uncle Tom's Cabin*, published on March 20, 1852, was the first American novel to reach sales of one million copies. Eventually extending to over a million.

Leonardo da Vinci's (1452 – 1519) *Mona Lisa* was originally titled *La Gioconda* for Lisa del Giocondo, wife of a wealthy Florentine silk merchant named Francesco del Giocondo.

Margin note in a book dated 1503, discovered [2005] in the library of the University of Heidelberg, Heidelberg, Baden-Württemberg, Germany, proved Lisa del Giocondo was the subject of *Mona Lisa*.
Courtesy: University Library of Heidelberg

French impressionist artist Paul Cézanne (1839-1906) taught his pet parrot to say, "Cézanne is a great painter!" for whenever a guest paid him a visit.

Victor Hugo's (1802 – 1885) *Les Miserables* [1862], with a word count of 823, contains the longest sentence in literature.

Victor Hugo, age 81
(1802 – 1885)
French author and poet
Photogravure courtesy: Charles F. Horne's
Great Men and Famous Women
Publisher: Selmar Hess, New York, 1894
[Photographer: Comte Stanislaw Julian Ostromóg Walery, 1830 – 1890]

British poet and playwright Ben Jonson (1572 – 1637) was branded with an "M" — for Murderer — on his left thumb for killing an actor in a duel [September 22, 1598]. He escaped the gallows by suffering this humiliation and forfeiting his "goods and chattels."

L. Frank Baum (1856 – 1919), author of *The Wonderful Wizard of OZ* [1900], named "OZ" from the "O" to "Z" file cabinet in his office.

In 1853 William Wells Brown (1814 – 1884) wrote *Clotel* [*The President's Daughter*], the first novel by an African-American. It was published in London, England.

Harriet Wilson (1825 – 1900) would write the first Afri-can-American novel published in the United States [1859].

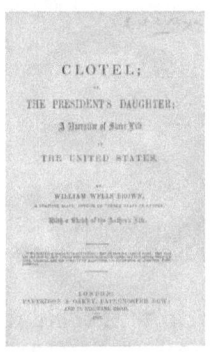

**Title page for William Wells Brown's (1814 – 1884)
novel *Clotel*, published by Partridge & Oakey,
London [1853].**
Courtesy:
University Library
University of North Carolina at Chapel Hill
CB #3900
208 Raleigh St.
Chapel Hill, NC 27514-8890

In 1899, the great American poet Carl Sandburg (1878 – 1967) was forced out of West Point for failing a grammar [and math] examination.

James M. Barrie (1860 – 1937), author of ***Peter Pan*** [appearing first in 1901 as a single volume], bequeathed all of the proceeds to his novel [1911] to London's Great Ormond

Street Hospital for Children.

**James Mathew Barrie in 1890-93
(1860 – 1937)
Author of *Peter Pan* [original book title:
Peter and Wendy, 1911].**
Courtesy: Victoria and Albert Museum, London

American Gothic, painted by Grant Wood (1891–1942), depicts the artists' sister Nan (1900 – 1990) and family dentist. Dr. B.H. McKeeby (1867 – 1950), as rural farm folk.

Nan Wood Graham and Dr. B.H. McKeeby in 1942.
Photo courtesy: Cedar Rapids Museum, Grand Rapids, MI

Ernest Hemingway (1899 – 1961) revised the last page of *A Farewell to Arms* a total of thirty-nine times [1929].

Artist Henri Matisse's (1869 – 1954) *La Bateau* hung upside down for 47 days in the Museum of Art, New York City before anyone noticed [1961]

Dr. Herman Tarnower (1910 – 1980), in his best-selling book *The Complete Scarsdale Medical Diet*, acknowledged the help of his friend Jean Harris, who would later kill him in a lovers' quarrel [March 10, 1980].

"The best thing about lying in bed late is that you learn to distinguish between first things and trivia, for whatever presses on you has to prove its importance before it makes you move."

Max Learner
(1902 – 1992)
American journalist and educator

Biblical Trivia

Did You Know:

Along the Dead Sea is a low salt mountain some biblical scholars believe is the pillar of salt Lot's wife was turned into following the destruction of Sodom and Gomorrah.

The Aramaic language of the ancient Bible did not have a translation for the phrase "many things." Usage for this term came down to us as "forty." Therefore, the "forty days" mentioned in both the Old and New Testament refers to "many days."

Dionysius Exiguus (ca 470 – ca 544),a 6th century monk,

originally created BC/AD as a biblical dating system in 525. Today, we use B.C.E. [Before the Common Era] and C.E. [Common Era] as a scholastic dating system.

The New Testament was originally written in Koine Greek [modern Greek] between ca 45 C.E. and ca 140 C.E.

The total population of the world at the time of Christ was approximately 250 million.

Approximately fifty men authored the Bible over a sixteen hundred-year period, dating from 1500 B.C.E. to over one hundred years after Christ.

Nicholas Breakspear (ca 1100 – 1159) was the only English pope [Adrian IV, 1154 – 1159].

The first Middle English translations of the Bible were initiated by John Wycliffe (ca 1320 – 1384) in 1382 and completed by his assistant, John Purvey (1353 – 1428) from 1388 to 1395.

The *Great Bible*, sanctioned by King Henry VIII of England in 1538, was the first authorized English version of the Bible published [1539], pre-dating the King James Bible by seventy-two years.

A Bible published in London in 1631 was known as the **Wicked Bible** because the word "not" was missing from the 7th Commandment, thus making it "Thou shalt commit adultery."

Also appearing in this Bible, though lesser known, is the passage: "The Lord hath shewed us his glory and **great arse**," instead of: "The Lord hath shewed us his glory and **greatness**." [Deuteronomy 5:24]

Approximately forty different authors wrote the sixty-six books of the King James Bible.

The Bible devotes five hundred verses on prayer, less than five hundred on faith, and over two thousand on money and possessions.

Although not named in the New Testament, traditional history cites the two thieves crucified with Jesus as Dismas and Gestes.

The first colony in the New World given a biblical name was Salem, Massachusetts.

The name "salem" stems from the Hebrew "shalom" and the Arabic "salam," which both mean "peace."

Comic Book Trivia

Did You Know:

Miscellaneous

The first modern comic book, which contained reprints of newspaper comic strips, was introduced by Eastern Color Printing in 1933, and offered free as a promotional gimmick for Proctor & Gamble Co.

So popular was this concept, the following year Eastern published a comic book entitled "Famous Funnies," selling it through the Woolworth's department chain for ten cents.

The rest, as we say, is history.

Detective Dick Tracy, modeled after Britain's Sherlock Holmes, first appeared in the *Detroit Free Press* on October

4, 1931.

Tracy's creator, Chester Gould (1900 – 1985), would in-troduce the comic world to innovative crime-fighting tech-nologies in use today.

Emil Blonsky, attempting to steal the research of Dr. Bruce Banner [the **Hulk**], accidentally exposed himself to a concentrated dose of gamma rays, transforming him into the green-skinned monster **Abomination**.

Though retaining his intelligence and personality, unlike the **Hulk**, Blonsky could not revert to human form.

Superman

Superman's full earthen name is commonly allowed as Clark **Joseph** Kent. [Although some sources claim it as Clark **Jerome** Kent in deference to creator Jerry Siegel.]

Jerry Siegel (1914 – 1996), with Joe Shuster (1914 – 1992) created Superman as a super-villain in 1933, but the character found itself repeatedly rejected until 1938, when *Detective Comics, Inc.* [National Periodicals Publications] took a chance on the revamped superhuman.

Superman and Lois Lane first kissed in *Superman* #3 [1940].

Although Lois had fallen in love with him from the very beginning of their relationship, it was not until the Man of Steel saved a town and her from a flood that she took the plunge.

Clark Kent was rejected from military service during World War II for failing the eye test portion of his physical.

Due to his X-ray vision, he inadvertently read an eye chart in the next room.

Superman's cousin, Supergirl, died in *Crisis on Infinite Earth* #7 [1985].

Superman was killed by **Doomsday**, an alien behemoth, in a special *Superman* #75 vol. II [October 1992 – November 1992].

Fortunately, he would later return in *Reign of the Supermen* [*Superman* #79 vol. II, June – October 1993].

Batman

Making its first appearance in *Detective Comics* #27 in May of 1939, 22-year-old comic artist Bob Kane (1915 – 1998) created Batman from four sources: Zorro; the mysterious Shadow; a 1930's movie *The Bat Whisperer*; Leonardo da Vinci's sketch of a man attempting flight with bat-like wings.

Batman's first Bat-villain was Catwoman. [*Batman* #1 in the Spring of 1940.]

Robin, the Boy Wonder was introduced in *Detective Comics* #38 in April of 1940.

His purpose, according to Kane, was simply to give Batman someone to talk to.

The original Batgirl, introduced in *Batman* #139 [Betty Kane] was the niece to Batwoman's Kathie Kane.

In a later version Batgirl was Barbara Gordon, daughter of Gotham City's Police Commissioner James Gordon.

Wonder Woman

Wonder Woman was created by psychologists William Moulton Marston (1893 – 1947) and Elizabeth Holloway Marston (1893 – 1993), co- inventors of the first lie detector [1917, systolic blood-pressure test. Forerunner of today's polygraph test.]

Wonder Woman first appeared in *All Star Comics* #8 [December 1941].
So popular was her character, she was given her own comic book the following year [***Wonder Woman*** #1].

Diana, princess of the Amazons, fell in love with American pilot Captain Steve Trevor, when he crash-landed on Paradise Island. She would accompany him back to "the world of man," where she would use her Amazonian powers as the crime-fighting Wonder Woman.

Wonder Woman's magic lasso was forged by the god Hephaestus from the Golden Girdle of Gaea, thus making it unbreakable with the added power to force those entrapped by it to tell the truth. [A concept based upon the Marstons' invention.]

The first issue of Gloria Steinem's *Ms.* Magazine [1972] featured Wonder Woman on its cover, with an article extolling the virtues of the world's leading female superhero.

Captain America

Captain America, first appearing in *Timely Comics* [predecessor to *Marvel Comics*] in 1940, was created by Joe Simon and Jack Kirby (1917 – 1994) to capitalize on America's oncoming patriotic sentiment toward her battle against Adolph Hitler's Nazism.

In March 1941, Captain America appeared in *Captain America* #1.

As a U.S. Armed Forces counterpart, Captain America would battle Nazi and Japanese troops.

The original shield carried by Captain America in *Captain America* #1 was badge-shaped. In *Captain America* #2 [April 1941] this would be replaced by the circular shape familiar to fans most recently.

Approximately one hour and thirty minutes into the 2008 *Iron Man* movie, Captain America's shield is seen in Tony Stark's workshop.

Captain America was brought to the screen on three separate occasions: 1. A 1944 serialized feature starring Dick Purcell (1908 – 1944) in the title role. 2. A 1979 made-for-TV movie, with Captain America played ineffectively by Reb Brown. 3. A 1992 direct-to-video movie, with Matt Sallinger as Captain America.

None were well received by viewers.

"I'm always trolling for trivia."
Lynn Abbey
American author

History Trivia

Did You Know:

The Code of Hammuradi (ancient Babylon) is the earliest surviving system of laws. Established between 1795 B.C.E. and 1750 B.C.E.

Of the Seven Wonders of the Ancient World, only the Great Pyramid of Giza [2560 B.C.E.] remains.

The lost Wonders are: the Hanging Gardens of Babylon [600 B.C.E], the Temple of Artemus at Ephesus [550 B.C.E.] the Statue of Zeus at Olympus [ca 433 B.C.E], the Mausoleum of Halicarnassus [353 – 350 B.C.E.], The Colossus of Rhodes [292 – 280 B.C.E] and the Lighthouse of Alexandria [built between 285 and 247 B.C.E.].

The Hanging Gardens of Babylon, one of the Seven Wonders of the Ancient World, was built by King Nebuchadnezza II (ca 630 – 562 B.C.E.) to please his homesick wife, Amyitis, who found the flat, barren terrain of Mesopotamia depressing compared to the lush vegetation of her homeland, Media.

Anaximander (ca 610 – 546 B.C.E.), a philosopher from Miletus, Greece is credited with making the first map of the known world around 550 B.C.E.

The concept of air conditioning stemmed from ancient Rome [ca 27 B.C.E.], where water from aqueducts circulated through certain houses to cool the enclosed areas.

Although expensive, the wealthy were willing to pay for this luxury. Times have never really changed.

Ancient Rome was the first city to reach a population of one million [5 B.C.E.].

It was not until 1800 C.E. that London, England would become the second city to reach that milestone.

When Mount Vesuvius erupted on August 24, 79 C.E., more than 2,000 Pompeiiani ran into cellars to await its end in safety

Excavators found their remains huddled together within these cavities nearly eighteen hundred years later.

The future St. Patrick (ca 387 – 461 C.E.) was originally brought to Ireland as a slave in 405 C.E.

Egbert of Wessex (? – 839), although not technically a "king," was proclaimed sole ruler of Britain in 829 C.E. for his powerful organizational skills and is thus considered by many scholars "the first king of England."

On October 17, 1469, Ferdinand II of Aragon (1469 – 1516) married Isabella I of Castile (1451 – 1504), which laid the foundation for the political unification of Spain by merging Aragon and Castile.

The Holy See's 134-man army, dating back to 1506, is the world's oldest guard unit.

King Henry VIII (1491 – 1547) of England introduced death by boiling and legalized extermination of [Roma] gypsies [1531].

Queen Elizabeth I (1533 – 1603) of England contracted smallpox at the age of 29, which left her face pockmarked and eventually her head nearly bald. She would wear heavy white [lead-based] make-up and various wigs throughout the years to disguise her disfigurement and loss.

Ann Smith Franklin (1696 – 1763), sister-in-law of Benjamin Franklin, was America's first woman newspaper editor [*Newport Mercury* of Newport, Rhode Island, 1762].

"Nothing of importance happened today," noted England's King George III (1738 – 1820) in his journal on July 4, 1776.

News of the Declaration of Independence first appeared in Philadelphia's German newspaper, *Pennsylvaninischer Skaatsbote*, on July 5, 1776. General George Washington (1732 – 1799) received the report on July 9th.

South Carolina statesman Henry Laurens' (1724 – 1792) was the first formal cremation in the United States [December 8, 1792], as per instructions in his will.

Queen Victoria of England (1819 – 1901) was the first monarch to live in Buckingham Palace [1837-1861].

The world's first adhesive postage stamp — known as the *Penny Black* — featuring the portrait of a young Queen Victoria (1819 – 1901) was introduced in Great Britain and Ireland on May 1, 1840.

Known as the *Penny Black*, this was the world's first adhesive postage stamp.
Courtesy:
National Postal Museum
2 Massachusetts Ave. N.E.
Washington, DC 20002

Elizabeth Blackwell (1821 – 1910) received the degree of Doctor of Medicine from the Medical Institute of Geneva College, New York on January 23, 1849, making her the first female to graduate from medical school in the United States.

In 1868, she founded a medical college to help other women achieve this goal.

**Elizabeth Blackwell in 1849
(1821 – 1910)
First female to graduate from
medical school in the United States.**
Photo courtesy:
National Institutes of Health
9000 Rockville Pike
Bethesada, Maryland 90892

Ulysses S. Grant (1822 – 1885) was president when *Uncle Sam* first "grew" his goatee [November 20, 1869].

Victoria Woodhull (1839 – 1927) was the first woman to

run for President of the United States [Equal Rights Party, 1872].

Victoria Woodhull, ca 1860
(1839 – 1927)
First woman to run for
President of the United States.
Photo courtesy: Library of Congress
[Photographer: Mathew Brady (1822 – 1896)]

George Armstrong Custer (1839 – 1876) elected to leave his four Gatling guns behind on June 25, 1876 [Battle of Little Big Horn].

New Haven, Connecticut was the first city in the United States to have a telephone directory [1878].

Fred White (1849 – 1880), first town marshal for Tombstone, Arizona and often depicted as elderly, was actually a 31-year-old lawman when shot [October 28,1880] and killed [died: October 30, 1880] by "cow-boys" gang member "Curly Bill" Brocius (ca 1845 – 1882).

French sculptor Frédéric-Auguste Bartholdi (1834-1904) used his wife for the body and his mother for the face in modeling the Statue of Liberty. [Dedicated to the United States from the people of France on October 28, 1886.]

Frédéric-Auguste Bartholdi in 1898
(1834 – 1904)
French sculptor
Creator of the Statue of Liberty
On February 18, 1879, he received
U.S. Patent #11,023 for "Design for
a Statue of Liberty Enlightening the World."
Photo courtesy: Library of Congress

William Kemmler (1860 – 1890) was the first prisoner to die by electrocution in the United States. [Auburn Prison, Auburn, New York, August 6, 1890.]

American women received the right to vote with ratification of the 19th Amendment to the United States Constitution on August 18, 1920.

Following a long exhaustive fight starting in 1848, the balance shifted in favor of women's suffrage in 1918 when President Woodrow Wilson [1913-21] changed his position, through his wife's careful influence, to support the amendment.

**Edith Bolling Galt Wilson
(1872 – 1961)
Woodrow Wilson's second wife
and First Lady [1915 – 1921].
Influential to President Wilson
and [unofficial] acting President of
United States [1919 – 1921] during her
husband's stroke and recuperation.**
Photo courtesy: Library of Congress

British Prime Minister Winston Churchill (1874 – 1965)

shared breakfast in bed with his pet parrot, Toby.

Romanian dictator, Nicolae Ceausescu (1918 – 1989), banned the game of *Scrabble* because it was too intellectual.

Holiday Trivia

Did You Know:

The first June Father's Day in the United States was celebrated in Spokane, Washington on June 19, 1910. However, it was not until 1966, by order of President Lyndon Johnson [1963- 65], that the third Sunday in June was proclaimed Father's Day; and still not officially recognized until it was signed into public law in 1972, during Richard Nixon's [1969- 74] administration.

Valentine's Day

The ancient Roman fertility festival of Lupercalia, commemorated annually on February 15th, is believed to have been the foundation for Valentine's Day.

Around 496 C.E. Pope Gelasius I [pope: 492 – 496], having renamed the pagan Lupercalia to St. Valentine's Day, moved it to February 14th.

It is believed by most scholars that Valentine's Day was named for a particular priest executed by Roman Emperor Claudius II (ca 214 – 269) around 269 C.E. for secretly performing marriages.

In a confusing decree, Claudius had outlawed marriage in a demented conviction that single men made for better soldiers.

Venus, the Goddess of Love, was purportedly the mother of Cupid, the mischievous winged child associated with Valentine's Day, whose arrows pierced the hearts of his victims, causing them to fall hopelessly in love with the first person they see.

Halloween

Although having several theories, it is generally accepted that Halloween dates back to an ancient Celtic New Year festival known as Samhain [pronounced Sow-in].

Believing the souls of those who had died during the year returned on the eve of Samhain to seek possession of living bodies throughout the following year, the Celts would deck out in ghoulish costumes and hold clamorous parties in their attempt to frighten away these invading spirits.

Hollowed-out turnips, fashioned in Ireland, were the first Jack-O'-Lanterns; with a piece of coal inserted to light the lamp.

According to legend an old man named Jack, who had tricked the devil, was barred from both heaven and hell upon his death and given this crude lamp to forever walk the earth in limbo.

When the Irish brought the Jack-O'-Lantern to America and applied it to the Halloween holiday, it was decided pumpkins were easier to carve.

Thanksgiving

The earliest feast of thanksgiving took place in Plymouth Colony [now Plymouth, Massachusetts] following the first harvest of 1621.

Squanto (? – 1623) of the Wampanoag Indians, who had

helped the pilgrim settlers survive the initial winter in the New World [1620], was honored at their first thanksgiving feast.

"The First Thanksgiving," Plymouth Colony 1621
[Painting by: Jean Leon Gerome Ferris (1863 – 1930)]
Courtesy: Library of Congress

The first national Thanksgiving Day was proclaimed by President George Washington [1789-97] on November 26, 1789.

Christmas

The real Saint Nicholas was born in Patara, near Myra in

modern Turkey around 270-280 C.E.

His kindness, as he traveled the countryside helping the sick and poverty-stricken by secretly gift-giving his inherited wealth, led to the legend of Santa Claus.

Eggnog, according to Captain John Smith (1580 – 1631) in his official reports, was first mixed and consumed in the Jamestown settlement of Virginia during its Christmas celebration of 1607.

"Nog" derived from "grog," which applies itself to any drink made from rum.

The first state in America to declare Christmas a legal holiday was Alabama [1836]. The last state was Oklahoma in 1907. [Note: Though some sources claim the date as 1890, Oklahoma did not become a state until November 16, 1907.]

Rudolph the Red-Nosed Reindeer was created by employee Robert L. May (1905 – 1976) for the Montgomery Ward chain of department stores as part of a widely publicized promotional gimmick in 1939.

This eventually led to a song of the same name, recorded by singing cowboy Gene Autry (1907 – 1998) in 1949, which was to become a Christmas classic.

"The roots of education are bitter, but the fruit is sweet."
Aristotle
(384 – 322 B.C.E.)
Greek philosopher

Inventions Trivia

Did You Know:

In 1775 British watchmaker Alexander Cummings was issued the first patent [English patent #814] for a flush toilet still in use today.

Thomas Jefferson (1743 – 1826) invented the first "hideaway bed" in America.

It was hoisted and secured to the ceiling when not in use.

[Note: Some sources question this, however, since no patent was ever taken out for a "hideaway bed" during Jefferson's lifetime. Yet, as a point of interest, Jefferson never held a patent for any of his twelve inventions.

The lawn mower was invented by Englishman Edward Beard Budding (1795 – 1846) in 1830, which advertised it as a "machine for the purpose of cropping or shearing the vegetable surface of lawns.

In 1857, Joseph C. Gayetty produced the first packaged bathroom tissue in the United States. Labeled *Gayetty's Medicated Paper*, it contained an abundance of a curative aloe additive and sold in packs of 500 sheets for fifty cents.

Gayetty's name was printed on each sheet.

The can opener was invented 48 years after the tin can. [Which was introduced in 1810].

In 1858, Ezra J. Warner of Waterbury, Connecticut patented a crude sickle-shaped instrument, which was eventually adopted by the United States military for exclusive use during the American Civil War [1861-65].

Before the advent of this little device, hungry men and women would attack the metal cans with hammers and chisels, knives and bayonets, even pistol and rifle fire. Often, when they finally pried open the pesky can, there was hardly any food left worth eating.

Writer Mark Twain (1835 – 1910) was granted a patent

for a self-pasting scrapbook [1872].

"No library is complete without a bible, Shakespeare, and Mark Twain's Scrapbook," exclaimed the *Norristown Herald* of Norristown, Pennsylvania in 1884.

Mark Twain in 1874
(1835 – 1910)
[Engraving from *Appleton's Journal* of July 4, 1874]
Appleton's *Journal* was a 19th century magazine of literature,
science and art, published from April 3, 1869 to December 1881.

When Alexander Graham Bell (1847 – 1922) blurted the words, "Mr. Watson, come here. I want you," on March 10, 1876, he was not testing his newly invented telephone. He had just spilled battery acid on his trousers and called his assistant, Thomas A. Watson (1854 – 1934), for help.

Watson picked up the words on the other end of the line and answered the summons.

[Note: This story may or may not be true. In the June 6, 2008 issue of *The New Yorker* magazine, Watson's great-great granddaughter claimed it a fabrication, "added to embellish the commonplace occasion of a new invention."]

At any rate, as this author quoted a well known publisher

in a previous work, "When fact disputes legend, print the legend."

Thomas Augustus Watson, ca 1883
(1854 – 1934)
He answered his employer's
desperate summons.
Courtesy:
University of Houston
4800 Calhoun Road.
Houston, TX 77004

Theophilus Van Kannel (1841 – 1919) designed the revolving door in 1888 to keep cold air out of office buildings. [Patented August 7, 1888.]

Socialite Josephine Garis Cochrane (1839 – 1913), tired of the servants chipping her fine china, once declared with disgust: "If nobody else is going to invent a dishwashing machine, I'll do it myself." And so she did. Obtaining a patent for the first commercially practical dishwasher on December 28, 1886 [patent #355,139].

Seven years later, her dishwasher received the top prize for inventions at the Columbian Exposition of 1893 [Chicago World's Fair].

In 1907, James Spengler invented the portable vacuum cleaner by placing together a soapbox [i.e. Large crate once used for packing and shipping bars of soap to merchants], pillowcase, a fan and tape.

Henry Ford (1863 – 1947) invented charcoal briquettes in the 1920s as a means of employing scrap wood left over in the manufacture of his Model T.

"Iron rusts from disuse? So does inaction sap the vigors of the mind."

Leonardo da Vinci
(1452 – 1519)
artist and inventor

Medical Trivia

Did You Know:

Greek physician Hippocrates (ca 460 – 370 B.C.E.) was the first to record case histories of patients.

In 1508, Leonardo da Vinci (1452 – 1519) suggested using contact lenses to improve vision.

Before gauze and cotton surgical dressings were introduced pressed sawdust was applied to wounds in American hospitals.

Western outlaw Jesse James (1849 – 1882) would blink uncontrollably at times due to a medical condition known as blepharospasms.

William Stewart Halsted (1852 – 1922) was the first surgeon to wear rubber gloves during an operation [1889].

Dr. Halsted had hired the Goodyear Rubber Company to develop and manufacture thin gloves that would not interfere with necessary sensitivity.

William Stewart Halsted
(1852 – 1922)
The first doctor to wear rubber
gloves during surgery. As a result,
he was known as "Mr. Clean" of medicine.
Photo courtesy: Library of Congress

Daniel David Palmer introduced chiropractic medicine in 1895.

Although considered a unique form of healing for the time, the principles of chiropractic therapy have been traced back to ancient Greece.

Famous aviator Charles A. Lindbergh (1902 – 1974), educated as a mechanical engineer, helped design a germ-free "artificial heart" in the early 1930s with French Nobel Prize -winning surgeon, Dr. Alexis Carrel (1874 – 1944).

Lindbergh and Carrel appeared together on the June 13, 1944 cover of *Time* magazine.

Portugal's Dr. Antonio Egas Moniz (1874 – 1955) was awarded a Nobel Prize in medicine for the now questionable prefrontal lobotomy [1949].

Dr. Richard H. Lawler (1896 – 1982) performed the first successful kidney transplant in 1950. Fifty-nine year old Ruth Tucker, the patient, lived for five years with her new kidney.

The swine flu vaccine of 1976 caused more death and illness than did the disease.

DSB [Drug-Seeking-Behavior]is a designation applied to

patients, or wannabe patients, who complain of a bogus ailment in an attempt to obtain narcotics.

Military Trivia

Did You Know:

The 9th century Chinese alchemists [Taoist monks] who discovered a way to produce gunpowder were in fact working on a formula for an elixir of immortality.

Patriots William Dawes (1745 – 1799) and Samuel Prescott (1751 – 1777) accompanied Paul Revere (1734 – 1818) on his celebrated midnight ride to warn the colonists of a British advance [April 18-19, 1775].

Both Dawes and Prescott remain relatively unknown today, since their names did not rhyme with Henry Wadsworth Longfellow's (1807 – 1882) opening line to his famous poem: "Come listen my children, and you shall hear..."

America's Revolutionary War ally, the French General Marquis de Lafayette (1759 – 1834), named his only son George Washington Lafayette (1779 – 1834).

American Civil War soldiers [Union] were the first to wear machine-made uniforms, thanks to the innovations of Isaac Merritt Singer (1811 – 1875) and Elias Howe (1819 – 1867) in their developments of the sewing machine.

Georgia was the last southern state to rejoin the Union after the American Civil War [July 18, 1870].

The second Boer War in South Africa [1899-1902] was the first conflict to have authorized film coverage.

The assassination of Austria's Archduke Franz Ferdinand on June 28, 1914, triggered World War I.

A German coded dispatch, known as the *Zimmerman Telegram*, was forwarded to Germany's ambassador to Mexico on January 19, 1917, instructing him to advise the Mexican government of their intent to restore the American southwest to them if they declared war on the United States.

This message was intercepted by British Naval Intelligence and decoded, however, which hastened President Woodrow Wilson's [1913-21] decision to enter into the war [April 1917].

On June 28, 1919, Germany signed for peace in the Palace of Versailles, near Paris.

Bridget Hitler (1891 – 1969), sister-in-law of German dictator Adolph Hitler, worked for the British war relief in New York City during World War II.

Bridget Dowling Hitler, 1941
(1891 – 1969)
She offered British war relief information
in New York City during World War II.
Photograph: New York World-Telegram and the Sun
[Newspaper published between: 1931-1966.]
Courtesy: Library of Congress

In 1944, Captain Ronald Reagan (1911 – 2004) signed Major Clark Gable's (1901 – 1960) army discharge papers.

The Battle of Okinawa [April 1, 1945 through June 1, 1945] was the last major battle of World War II, leading to the A-bomb attacks on Hiroshima and Nagasaki and surrender of Japanese forces on August 10, 1945.

The Soviet Union declared war on Japan [August 8, 1945] two days before the Japanese agreed to surrender unconditionally.

During the Korean War [on April 11, 1951] President Harry S. Truman [1945-53] removed General Douglas MacArthur (1880 – 1964) from command of the United Nations forces and replaced him with the less argumentative General Mathew Bunker Ridgeway (1895 – 1993).

Dwight David Eisenhower (1890 – 1969) was president when major Korean War combat operations ceased on July 27, 1953. [The conflict has never officially ended.]

The first official United States casualties of the Vietnam War were Major Dale R. Buis (1921 – 1959) and Master Sergeant Chester M. Ovnand (1914 – 1959), on the afternoon of July 8, 1959.

The Vietnam War officially ended on April 30, 1975 at 8:35 a.m., when ten Marines departed the United States Embassy in Saigon.

By 11:00 a.m. that morning, the red and blue Viet Cong flag flew from Saigon's Presidential Palace and General Doung Van Minh (1916 – 2005), South Vietnam's new president, broadcast a message of unconditional surrender.

"The next best thing to knowing something is knowing where to find it."

Samuel Johnson
(1709 – 1784)
English author, essayist and poet

Miscellaneous Trivia

Did You Know:

Vanilla, followed by chocolate, is the most preferred flavor.

The Oak tree is most often struck by lightning.

Bathing caps were invented to prevent clogged drains.

German Shepherds bite the most humans.

The soccer ball has 32 leather panels, which are held together with 642 stitches.

Billionaire Howard Hughes (1905 – 1976) was the only person to pilot his monstrously heavy airplane, the **Spruce Goose** [1947].

The Brooklyn Dodgers signed Jackie Robinson (1919 – 1972) to the major leagues in 1947, ending nearly eight years of baseball segregation.

Pinto Colvig (1892 – 1969) was the original voice of "Bozo the Clown," recorded on a 1946 album, which accompanied a first of its kind read-along book.

German physician Emil von Behring (1854 – 1917) won the first Nobel Prize for Medicine in 1901 for his work on serum therapy against diphtheria.

When a bar of soap was purchased before 1831, the grocer would hack off a chunk from a large block.

Robert E. Peary (1856 – 1920) is arguably the first person to have reached the North Pole [April 6, 1909].

Robert E. Peary
(1856 – 1920)
North Pole explorer
Photo courtesy:
U.S. National Oceanic and
Atmospheric Administration
1401 Constitution Ave, NW
Washington DC 20230

Coin banks are commonly pig-shaped, stemming from frugal savers in the 18th century placing their money in earthenware jars of dense orange clay known as pyggs.

World War II is still not technically over. Germany and the Soviet Union have never signed a formal peace treaty.

On October 24,1901, Annie Edson Taylor (1838 – 1921) was the first person to go over Niagara Falls in a barrel and escape unhurt.

Annie Edson Taylor, 1901
(1838 – 1921)
Standing next to her famous barrel.
Photo courtesy:
Francis J. Petre Collection
Niagara Falls Public Library
1425 Main Street
Niagara Falls, NY 14395

Some shoes squeak because two layers of leather in the sole are rubbing together.

A simple solution is to drive a tack through the sole to remove the squeak.

King George III (1738 – 1820) of England granted a royal charter to the New York City Chamber of Commerce in

1770, making it the oldest chamber of commerce in the United States.

Hatbands trace back to medieval knights wearing a lady-love's scarf around their helmets.

Gustave Eiffel (1832 – 1923), builder of the Eiffel Tower, also designed the right arm and full steel structure supporting the Statue of Liberty.

Alexandre Gustave Eiffel, 1893
(1832 – 1923)
French structural engineer
Famous for designing the Eiffel Tower.
Courtesy: Library of Congress

Abraham Lincoln (1809 – 1865), Franklin D. Roosevelt (1882 – 1945) and Dwight D. Eisenhower (1890 – 1969) used the pronoun "I" only once in their inaugural speeches. However, in 1901, Theodore Roosevelt (1858 – 1919) was the only U.S. President in history [as of this writing] to deliver an entire inaugural address without saying "I."

Fourteen years before the **Titanic** sank on the night of April 14, 1912, novelist Morgan Robertson (1861 – 1915) published *Futility*. The story of an ocean liner named **Titan** that struck an iceberg on an April night.

Montgomery Ward was the first company in the United States to offer "Satisfaction guaranteed or your money back," in their mail order catalog of 1875 [catalog #13; Spring and Summer, 1875].

Mr. Potato Head was the first toy advertised on television in the United States [1952].

Felix the Cat was the first cartoon character made into a balloon for Macy's Thanksgiving Day Parade [1927]. In that year, air filled this first balloon. However, in 1928, Helium was introduced into the expanding cast.

Popeye's Olive Oyl was the first female cartoon character balloon in Macy's Thanksgiving Day Parade [1982].

Alice Stebbins Wells (1873 – 1957) was the first female police officer in the United States.

Sworn into the Los Angeles Police Department on September 12, 1910, she was later issued "Policewoman Badge Number One."

Alice Stebbins Wells
(1873 – 1957)
First policewoman in the United States.
Founder:
International Association of Policewomen [1915].
Photo courtesy:
Los Angeles Police Department
150 N. Los Angeles St.
Los Angeles, CA 90012

The word "assassination" was coined by William Shakespeare (1564 – 1616) in *Macbeth* Act I, Scene VI.

Broadcast historians generally recognize *Professor Quiz*, airing in 1936, as the first **true** quiz show on radio [CBS radio network].

Wrigley's Juicy Fruit chewing gum was the first product scanned by barcode [June 26, 1974].

Pepsi-Cola was originally named Brad's Drink [1898] for its inventor, pharmacist Caleb Davis Bradham (1867 – 1934).

Chef Caesar Cardini (1896 – 1956) created the Caesar Salad in 1924 at his Tijuana, Mexico restaurant.

Gennaro Lombardi of New York City opened the first pizzeria in the United States [1905].

Ten percent of men in the world are left-handed, while only eight percent are women.

English model and actress, Lesley Hornby (better known

as "Twiggy"), was nicknamed "Sticks" in her childhood.

Although Peter Mark Roget (1779 – 1869), a 19th century English Physician, devised his thesaurus to allow for students to find the correct word for the proper situation, he is also credited with developing a mathematical tool called the log-log slide rule, used exclusively until advent of the electronic calculator.

A Canadian stagecoach robber known as "The Gentleman Bandit" (Bill Miner, ca 1847 – 1913) is credited to have created the classic holdup line "Hands up."

**Ezra Allen "Bill" Miner
(ca 1847 – 1913)
Dubbed "The Gentleman Bandit."**
Photo courtesy:
R.C.M.P. [Royal Canadian Mounted Police] Archives
Ottawa, Canada

Famous comedian/actor/ singer, Jimmy Durante (1893 –

93

1980), had his nose insured for $140, 000.

The average lifespan of the Stone Age cave dweller was eighteen years.

Robert L. Ripley (1890 – 1949), of *Ripley's Believe It or Not!* fame, was the first inductee into the **National Trivia Hall of Fame** [1980], sponsored by *Trivia Unlimited* Magazine [published: 1979-84].

America's famous writer, humorist and homemaker, Erma Bombeck (1927 – 1996), once requested her epitaph to read: "BIG DEAL! I'm used to dust."

History's first known author was a woman [High Priestess] named Enheduana [En-he-du-ana], who lived in Southern Mesopotamia [ca 2300 – 2225 B.C.E.].

Alabaster disks bearing her name, along with poem fragments, were discovered in the 1920s during British archaeologist Sir Charles Leonard Wooley's (1880 – 1960) excavations at Ur in Mesopotamia.

Lady Godiva (? – 1080) rode naked through the streets of Coventry,England on horseback to persuade her husband,

Leofric (968 – 1057), Earl of Mercia, to reduce oppressive taxes.

Napoléon I (1769 – 1821) of France originally designed the present national flag of Italy in 1805.

Switzerland, Austria, France and Slovenia border Italy.

According to the 1890 Bureau of Census records, farming stood as the most common occupation in the United States.

An estimated average of twenty-five people jump from San Francisco's Golden Gate Bridge per year.

These are bodies recovered, however, and do not reflect those swept out to sea.

Austin, Texas is the southernmost state capital in the 48 contiguous United States.

The 100 Years War between two royal houses competing for the French throne lasted 116 years [1337 – 1453].

American poet Julia Ward Howe (1819 – 1910), author of *The Battle Hymn of the Republic*, first proposed a special day for mothers in 1872. President Woodrow Wilson [1913-21], through the influence of First Lady Ellen Axson Wilson [1913-14], proclaimed the national observance of Mother's Day on Sunday, May 9, 1914.

[Note: Although Mrs. Howe wrote the *Mother's Day Proclamation* in 1870, she officially proposed it as assistant editor of *Women's Journal* in 1872.]

Julia Ward Howe, ca 1861
(1819 – 1910)
poet, abolitionist, social activist
Made the first Mother's Day proposal.
Portrait courtesy:
Julia Ward Howe, 1819 – 1910 by Laura E.
Richards (1850 – 1943) and Maud Howe
Eliot (1854 – 1948), assisted by Florence
Howe Hall (1845 – 1922)
[Published: Houghton Mifflin Company
Boston and New York, 1915]

The wingspan of a Boeing 747 [195', 8"] is longer than the Wright Brothers' famous first flight of December 17, 1903 [120'].

The *Ancon* was the first ship to travel through the Panama Canal [August 15, 1914].

The ancient Olympic games lasted from 776 B.C.E until 393 C.E., when they were abolished by Roman Emperor Theodosius I (347 – 395 C.E.).

On average, a person eats eight spiders while sleeping during his/her lifetime.

Chief Sitting Bull's father was named Jumping Bull.

The month of August has the most birthdays, while the most popular day of birth for any month is Tuesday. [According to the National Center for Health Services, Hyattsville, MD 20782.]

Mormon leader Brigham Young (1801 – 1877) had fifty-seven children with sixteen of his twenty-seven conjugal wives.

Vermont entered the Union as the 14th state on March 4, 1791.

The first recorded major eastern United States earthquake occurred in the city of Charleston, SC on August 31, 1886. [9:50 p.m. and lasting 1 minute.]

Cats and dogs, as with people, favor either their left or right side. They are left or right-pawed, according to tests conducted by The Institute for the Study of Animal Problems in Washington, DC.

Movies Trivia

Did You Know:

The famous American "tough guy" stage and film actor James Cagney's (1899 – 1986) first theatrical performance was as a chorus girl in a show called *Every Sailor* [1919].

The first British sound film was director Alfred Hitchcock's (1899 – 1980) 1929 classic, *Blackmail*.

Child star Shirley Temple was three years old when she appeared in her first movie series [called "shorts'], *Baby Burlesks* [1932].

British actor David Niven (1910–1983) made his American screen debut as a Mexican wearing a blanket in the first *Hopalong Cassidy* movie [1935].

He would later laughingly quip: "Of course, they daren't let me open my mouth."

The great Palomino Trigger (1932 – 1965), then known as Golden Cloud, was ridden by Olivia de Haviland in *The Adventures of Robin Hood* [1938] before singing cowboy actor Roy Rogers (1911 – 1998) rode him into silver screen history.

Humphrey Bogart (1899 – 1957) appeared as a zombie in a 1939 horror movie called *The Return of Dr. X.*

Though said to be a coincidence, trivia rumor has it that Sesame Street's "odd couple" Ernie and Bert were named after the taxi driver [Ernie] and policeman [Bert] of Frank Capra's *It's a Wonderful Life* [1946].

Charles Buchinsky played Vincent Price's (1911 – 1993) henchman Igor in the 3-D classic, *House of Wax* [1953],before changing his name to Charles Bronson (1921 – 2005).

Actor Humphrey Bogart's (1899 – 1957) ashes are in an urn, which also contains a small gold whistle inscribed with the words his actress wife [Lauren Bacall] delivered to him in their first movie together, *To Have and Have Not*: "If you need anything, just whistle." [1944]

Norman Bates, in Robert Block's (1917 – 1994) novel *Psycho* [1959] and Alfred Hitchcock's (1899 – 1980) horror film of the same name [1960], was based on serial killer Edward Gein (1906 – 1984).

Colonel Harlan Sanders (1890 – 1980), famous for his Kentucky Fried Chicken restaurants, once appeared in four feature movies as himself [1967-70].

The brighter you are, the more you have to learn."
Don Herald
(1889 – 1966)
American humorist

Mythology Trivia

Did You Know:

In Greek mythology, the Titan Prometheus created mankind from clay.
In Roman mythology, it was the goddess Cura.

In Greek mythology, Iris was the goddess of the rainbow.

Hel was the goddess of the underworld in Norse mythology.

Ares, the Greek god of war, was the only son of Zeus and Hera.

In his rampage across the heavens and earth, he was often accompanied by his sister Eris [goddess of strife] and his sons Deimos [god of terror] and Phobos [god of fear].

In Hebrew traditional records, Lilith was the first wife of Adam, whose refusal to submit to her husband's sexual positioning demands estranged her from the Garden of Eden.

As Eve, Adam's second wife, moved in, Lilith winged her way into mythological history as the vampiric Queen of the Night.

Greek mythology asserts the Titan Prometheus to have accorded mortals the use of fire.

A Greek legend, passed down through the ages, alleges that a skilled woodworker named Epeius was commissioned by Odysseus to build the Trojan horse, which put an end to the ten-year war.

Arges, Brontes and Steropes were the Cyclops brothers

in Greek mythology. [Hesiod's ***Theogony***, ca 700 B.C.E.]

Helios, the Greek sun god, was portrayed as the Colossus of Rhodes [forerunner to America's Statue of Liberty], which stood more than one hundred feet high, and constructed as one of the wonders of the ancient world between 292 and 280 B.C.E.

Unfortunately, this grand structure was demolished when a devastating earthquake struck Rhodes in 226 B.C.E.

Colossus of Rhodes
This illustration may be a fanciful depiction,
since no one knows for sure where the structure stood before its destruction in 226 B.C.E.
Artwork from:
The Book of Knowledge, The Grolier Society, 1911
Courtesy:
The Grolier Club
47 E. 60th St.
New York, NY 10022

Although today's accepted opinions have perpetuated an

idea that sunlight can destroy the mythological vampire, ancient vampirian tradition claims cremation by "the fire of a torch" as the foremost method of destruction.

Political Trivia

Did You Know:

The First Continental Congress met secretly from September 5, 1774 to October 26, 1774 in Philadelphia, Pennsylvania [Carpenter's Hall] to protest the Intolerable Acts imposed by England's King George III (1738 – 1820) as punishment for the Boston Tea Party. Every colony but Georgia sent representatives to the Congress.

The first vice president of the United States was John Adams [1789-97].

Of the three United States presidents who died on Independence Day, Thomas Jefferson (1743 – 1826) died first.

John C. Calhoun (1782 – 1850) was the first United States vice president to resign from office [December 28, 1832].

Interestingly, he was the first vice president born a United States citizen.

John Augustus Roebling (1806 – 1869), political reformer and engineer most famously recognized for designing New York's Brooklyn Bridge [actually completed by his son, Washington Augustus Roebling (1837 – 1926) and opened in 1883], developed the first successful wire cable suspension bridge in America [*Allegheny Aqueduct Bridge*, Pittsburgh, Pennsylvania, 1844-45].

John Augustus Roebling
(1806 – 1869)
Designer of the *Allegheny Aqueduct Bridge*.
[1844-45]
Artwork courtesy: Library of Congress

Scottish novelist and poet Sir Walter Scott (1771 – 1832) entered the political world by extending words from his famous poem *The Lady of the Lake* to help arrange America's presidential anthem, *Hail to the Chief.*

Set to music by Englishman James Sanderson (1769 – 1841) around 1810, it was first individually performed to announce the arrival of President James Knox Polk [1845-49] at his inauguration of March 4, 1845.

Julia Gardiner Tyler (1820 – 1889), the wife of Polk's predecessor John Tyler (1790 – 1862), had previously suggested its accompaniment whenever an American president made a public appearance.

It was not, however, officially recognized as a musical presidential tribute in the eyes the United States Department of Defense [formally the Department of War and the governing body for such affairs] until 1954.

Chorus sheet to *Hail to the Chief*
Composed by James Sanderson
Courtesy: National Archives and Records Administration

When Andrew Jackson (1767 – 1845) ran for the presidency in 1828, his opponents labeled him a "jackass" for his political views. Thereupon Jackson, who loved controversy, had a picture of a donkey painted on his campaign posters.

The donkey, however, was not widely regarded as a democratic mascot until political editorial cartoonist Thomas Nast (1840 – 1902) first depicted the animal in an 1870 issue of *Harper's Weekly*.

The elephant was officially accepted as the Republican symbol when Thomas Nast again took up his pen to fashion the pachyderm in the 1874 issue of *Harper's Weekly*.

Thomas Nast's political cartoon of 1874, showing an elephant labeled: "The Republican Vote."
Courtesy: National Archives and Records Administration

In 1903, Mother Jones [Mary Harris Jones, 1830 – 1930] organized the "March of the Mill Children" to demand an end to child labor.

The march, consisting of Jones and several dozen children, of whom many were crippled by machinery in textile mills, trekked from Philadelphia to President Theodore Roosevelt's [1901- 09] summer home on Long Island.

Although Roosevelt refused to see them, their march would draw national attention and lead to the passing of child labor laws.

On December 16, 1922, mentally-deranged Polish painter and art critic Eligiusz Niewiadomski (1869 – 1923) assasinated Poland's first president Gabriel Narutowicz (1865 – 1922) for his political beliefs.

He was captured, tried, sentenced to death, and executed on January 31, 1923.

Famous strongman and mail order bodybuilding entrepreneur, Charles Atlas (1892 – 1972), posed for the statue of Alexander Hamilton that fronts the Treasury Building in Washington, DC.

Calvin Coolidge (1872 – 1933), affectionately known as

"Silent Cal," refused to use his office telephone while president [1923-29]. "If you don't say anything," he once quipped, "you won't be called on to repeat it."

Swiss carpenter and clock-maker, Johann Georg Elser (1903 – 1945), attempted to assassinate Germany's despotic ruler, Adolph Hitler (1889 – 1945), on November 8, 1939 at Bürgerbraukeller Hall with a time bomb. However, Hitler left the building thirteen minutes prior to the explosion.

Elser was arrested in an escape attempt, imprisoned in the Sachsenhausen Concentration Camp and later Dachau, where the SS executed him just twenty-seven days before V-E Day. [Victory in Europe Day, May 7-8, 1945. Germany's *Act of military surrender* was signed in Reims, France on May 7th and on May 8th in Berlin, Germany.]

Science Trivia

Did You Know:

India ink was developed in Neolithic China [middle 3rd millennium B.C.E.].

The idea of the atom was first introduced by Leucippus (ca 500 – 450 B.C.E.) of Miletus, Greece near the end of his life in 450 B.C.E.

Theorizing that all material consisted of bits of matter too small to be seen, Leucippus believed atoms [from the Greek "atomos"] were the building blocks of all temporal bodies and therefore unable to be broken down further.

Greek philosopher Aristotle (384 – 322 B.C.E.) reasoned the world was round long before Columbus.

German scientific hobbyist and gunsmith August Kotter brought the rifle into existence in 1520. Soon after, he sold his design to several manufacturers who made small moderations for their own-patented use.

Plus and minus ["equal"] signs were first introduced by Welsh physician and mathematician Robert Recorde (1510 – 1558) in 1557.

Physicist and astronomer Galileo Galilei (1564 – 1642) began the study of physics shortly after noticing a chandelier swinging during a 1581 earthquake.

Galileo Galilei first saw the moons of Jupiter through his telescope on January 7, 1610.

Galileo Galilei, after being forced by the Roman Catholic Church to declare the Earth motionless, muttered: "Nevertheless, it does move." Thereupon, the Church Inquisition placed him under house arrest for the remainder of his life.

In 1642, 19-year-old French genius Blaise Pascal (1623 – 1662) invented a mechanical adding machine [Pascal's calculator] to help his tax commissioner father in his work.

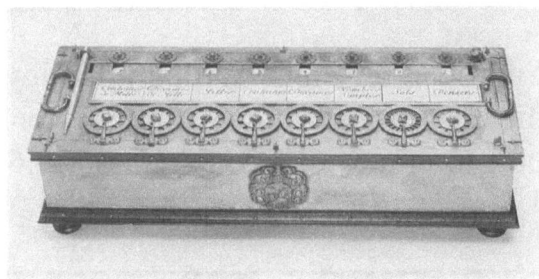

Pascal's calculator [Pascaline]
Invented by:
Blaise Pascal
(1623 – 1662)
An early mechanical calculator.
Courtesy:
Musée des arts et métiers – Cnam
292, rue Saint-Martin
75141 Paris Cedex 03 – France

English mathematician Charles Babbage's (1791 – 1871) concept of the Analytical Engine in 1833 [programmed to store calculations through "punch cards"] was the basis for today's computer.

Swedish engineer Immanuel Nobel (1801 – 1872), father of the more famous Alfred Nobel (1833 – 1896), invented the rotary lathe, which led to the development of modern plywood in the mid 19th century.

In 1885, American physicist William Stanley, Jr. (1858 – 1916) built the first transformer to transfer current of one electrical circuit to another [U.S. Patent #349,611, September 21, 1886].

German scientific researcher Wilhelm Conrad Röentgen (1845 – 1923) named his discovery of invisible beams X-rays because he had no idea what the mysterious rays were. This find would earn him the first Nobel Prize in Physics [1901].

Frederick Wells found the Cullinan Diamond, the largest rough gem-quality diamond ever discovered, on January 25, 1905.

Its original carets were cut for the British Crown Jewels and the British royal family's collection.

When newspaperman William Randolph Hearst (1863 –

1951) sent a telegram to a foremost astronomer with the question: "Is there life on Mars? Please cable one thousand words," he received the reply: "Nobody knows," repeated five hundred times.

The remains of a hobbit-like human, standing no higher than a meter, was discovered on the island of Flores, Indonesia in 2004 and dated to have lived as recently as 13,000 years ago; shattering the belief that homosapiens alone lived on earth for the past 25,000 years.

Natural gas is odorless. The rotten-egg smell is artificially added as a safety measure to detect leaks.

Those in the pharmacy profession refer to sleeping pills as "pillows."

"A weak mind is like a microscope, which magnifies trifling things but cannot receive great ones."
Lord Chesterfield
(1694 – 1773)
British statesman

Space Trivia

Did You Know:

Current astronomical observations suggest our universe is 13.73 billion years old and is in constant expansion. [NASA's Wilkinson Microwave Probe]

The core of our sun is 27,000 degrees Fahrenheit, while its surface is merely 10,000 degrees Fahrenheit.

Only 55% of Americans surveyed know the sun is a star.

Contrary to what many believe, the sun is the only star in

our solar system.

Saturn, having the least density of all the planets in our solar system, would float if placed in a tub full of water. [Yes, it would have to be a big tub!]

Of all the planets in our solar system, Earth is the only one not named for a Roman god or goddess.

Venus, as the brightest planet viewed from Earth, is often referred to as the "Evening Star" when seen in the west and the "Morning Star" when in the east.

Neptune is seen to have dark ovals on its surface, which astronomers believe are hurricane-like storms [*Voyager 2* space probe, 1989].

Since the Milky Way is believed approximately 100,000 light-years in diameter and our solar system is 26,000 light-years from the center of the Galaxy, it would take our sun 250 million years to pull us through one revolution around the center of the Milky Way. [Note: All small objects in the Milky Way revolve around the larger Galaxy's center.]

A light-year travels 9,500,000,000,000 kilometers,which is the distance light travels in one year. [Note: A kilometer equals 0.6214 miles.]

Scientist Robert H. Goddard (1882 – 1945) fired the first rocket using liquid propellant, which would initiate the idea of a practical space program, on March 16, 1926.

Dr. Robert H. Goddard
(1882 – 1945)
Dr. Robert Goddard launched his rocket on
March 16, 1926, at Auburn, Massachusetts.
Photo courtesy:
NASA Headquarters
300 E Street SW
Washington, DC 20024

The word astronaut in Latin means, "star sailor."

From thousands of applications presented within every two years, NASA accepts one hundred possible astronauts and narrows it down to a final selection of twenty.

Neil Armstrong, the first human to walk on the moon, stepped his left foot from the Lunar module "Eagle" onto its surface on July 20, 1969.

The plaque left on the moon by Apollo 11 lunar module "Eagle" reads: "Here men from the planet Earth first set foot upon the Moon July 1969 A.D. / WE CAME IN PEACE FOR ALL MANKIND."

Astronaut Alan Sheppard (1923 – 1998) is the only person, to date, to have played golf on the surface of the moon [1971].

Today's spacesuits are made with interchangeable parts so that more than one astronaut can fit them for use.

Television Trivia

Did You Know:

The comedy team of Dean Martin (1917 – 1995) and Jerry Lewis shared $200 for their appearance on the first *Ed Sullivan Show* [*Toast of the Town*] in June of 1948.

The first coast-to-coast network television program was *Kukla, Fran and Ollie* [1949].

James Dean (1931 – 1955), as a struggling young actor, tested stunts for the *Beat the Clock* TV quiz show [1951].

Future *Odd Couple* co- stars Tony Randall (1920 –2004) and Jack Klugman first met on the soundstage of *Captain Video and His Video Rangers*, an early children's television show [1949 – 1955].

The only words spoken by Clarabell the Clown on *The Howdy Doody Show* was "Good-bye, kids" on the last episode [2,343rd], September 30, 1960.

In the original script for the *Star Trek* television series, the U.S.S Enterprise was named U.S.S. Yorktown [1964].

Actor Telly Savalas (1924 – 1994), famous as the cool detective *Kojak*, first shaved his head for the role of Pontius Pilate in the 1965 movie *The Greatest Story Ever Told*.

Gary Burghoff played *Peanuts'* comic strip character Charlie Brown in the Broadway musical *You're a Good man, Charlie Brown* [1967], before movie and TV viewers would recognize him as Cpl. Radar O'Riley of *M*A*S*H*.

The Flying Nun TV sitcom [1967-70], starring a young

Sally Field in the title role, was based on the heartwarming novel *The Fifteenth Pelican* by Tere Rios (1917 – 1999).

Crooner/actor Bing Crosby (1903 – 1977) turned down the role of *Colombo* in the movie pilot [1968] and television detective series [1971-78], allowing Peter Falk to catapult to stardom as the lovable, absent-minded police lieutenant.

Johnny Carson (1925 – 2005) delivered 4,531 monologues during his thirty years as host of *The Tonight Show*.

Don Johnson played Elvis Presley (1935 – 1977) in the 1981 made-for-TV movie *Elvis and the Beauty Queen*.

Funny woman Phyllis Diller is known to have delivered twelve punch lines a minute, six more than rapid-fire comedian Bob Hope (1903 – 2003).

Tony Randall (1920 – 2004), the faultless neat freak Felix Unger in the *Odd Couple* TV sitcom [1970-75] once noted in an article, "I am a slob, but nobody will believe me."

When asked by a reporter what he would like his epitaph to read, TV host Johnny Carson (1925 – 2005) replied: "I'll be right back,"

U.S. Presidents Trivia

Did You Know:

Samuel Huntington (1731 – 1796) was elected President of the Continental Congress on September 28, 1779 and, by ratification of the Articles of Confederation on March 1, 1781, became the first President of the United States in Congress Assembled, serving until July 9, 1781.

George Washington (1732 – 1799) was not sworn into the presidency of the United States until April 30, 1789.

George Washington's [1789-97] second inaugural address was the shortest in United States history, containing 135 words and lasting two minutes [March 4, 1793].

During the presidential campaign of 1800, Thomas Jefferson (1743 – 1826) craved the office to such a degree he hired tabloid-type reporter James Thomas Callender (1758 – 1803) to write [false] negative articles on his one-time friend, incumbent President John Adams [1797-1801], accusing him of consorting with British mistresses.

Jefferson won the election, but refused to honor his commitment to appoint Callender postmaster of Richmond, Virginia. Thereupon, Callender published stories that Jefferson sired a number of children by his mulatto slave Sally Hemings (ca 1773 – 1835). Opening a controversy still debated today.

James Madison (1751 – 1836), 4th President of the United States [1809-17], was the smallest president at 5' 4" tall and never weighing more than 100 lbs.

Former president, Andrew Jackson (1767 – 1845), requested he be entombed with a copy of the United States Constitution placed under his head.

The Panic of 1837, which led to a five-year depression of bank failures and record high unemployment, was publically held accountable to"Old Kinderhook" President Martin Van Buren [1837-41].

Although this panic and subsequent depression may have been the effects of Van Buren's refusal to involve the government in banking issues, their causes purportedly stemmed from his predecessor's [Andrew Jackson, 1828-37] speculative economic policies.

When Vice-President John Tyler (1790 – 1862) ventured to assume the office of president [1841-45] following the death of President William Henry Harrison on April 4, 1841, he was crippled by a confused process of succession for two days, unable to affect full power until April 6, 1841.

It was not until 1967 that the 25th Amendment made clear the full process of succession to the United States Presidency.

President Franklin Pierce [1853-57] was former First Lady Barbara Pierce Bush's great-great-great uncle.

James Buchanan (1791 – 1868), 15th President of the United States [1857-61], had the opportunity to purchase Cuba for $90,000,000. Congress, however, having little trust for the strange, bachelor president refused to grant him the money, fearing he would "take the currency and run."

So frustrated was he with this and similar troubling issues with Congress, he wrote a note to the newly elected Abraham Lincoln in 1860: "My dear sir. If you are as happy on entering the presidency as I am on leaving it, you are a happy man indeed." [Note: There are several variants to this particular Buchanan sentiment. It was left to this author to choose what he thought the best rendering.]

Abraham Lincoln (1809 – 1865) was the first president to appear on a U.S. coin [1909].

Abraham Lincoln
(1809 – 1865)
[President: 1861-65]
This photo, taken on February 9, 1864,
was chosen for the "Lincoln penny."
Courtesy: Library of Congress
[Photographer: Anthony Berger, Mathew Brady's Studio]

Having been diagnosed with terminal throat cancer in 1884, former President Ulysses S. Grant [1869-77] would regularly swab the inside of his neck with cocaine, which allowed him to counteract the effects of pain-dulling and sleep-inducing morphine prescribed by his doctor. This enabled him in the race to finish his memoirs for the financial benefit of his destitute wife and family, since he knew he would not live another year.

At 8:06 a.m., July 23, 1885, while looking over a final draft of the manuscript, he laid it aside, asked for a glass of water, and died.

The volume had been completed a few days before his death and enthusiastically promoted by iconic author Mark Twain (1835 – 1910), earning the Grant family $450, 000.

[Note: Morphine was, and still is in most cases, a legal pain-relieving medication. Cocaine was an ingredient often used in prescription medicines of the 19th century and earlier. Neither was declared illegal until they had been abused.]

On March 30, 1867, Secretary of State William Seward [1861-69] completed purchase of 586,412 square miles of a frozen, barren land from the Russian Empire for 2 cents [$7,200,000] an acre.

Mocked as "Seward's Folly" by both the American public and many associated with Andrew Johnson's administration [1865-69], Alaska would emerge as a vital and prosperous territory and state.

Today, Alaska celebrates its purchase on the last Monday of March, as *Seward's Day*. Still, even though Seward implemented Alaska's purchase, we must applaud President Andrew Johnson's (1808 –1875) courage in approving the project.

Alexander Graham Bell (1847 – 1922) invented a metal-detecting device to locate the bullet lodged in President James Abram Garfield [1881-81] after he was shot in the back by disgruntled office-seeker Charles Guiteau (1841 – 1882) in July of 1881.

Unfortunately, it failed to work due to interference from Garfield's steel-spring mattress and the bullet remained in the president's body until he died on September 19, 1881.

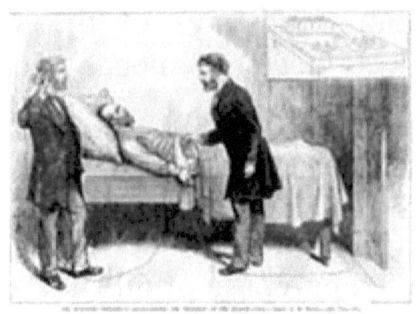

**Alexander Graham Bell' s metal-locating device tried un-
successfully to find the bullet lodged in President Garfield.**
Courtesy:
National Museum of American History
14th Street and Constitution Avenue NW
Washington, DC

A reformed bachelor, Grover Cleveland (1851 – 1908) was the first president [1885-89, 1893-97] married in the Executive Mansion [Frances Folsom. (1864 – 1947, m.1886] and the only president to have a child born there [Esther Cleveland, 1893 – 1980].

Benjamin Harrison (1833 – 1901) was president [1889-93] when electricity was installed in the Executive Mansion in 1891. However, he and the First Lady feared being zapped by the switches, so refused to use it.

The horse ridden by future president, Theodore "Teddy" Roosevelt (1858 – 1919), in the Battle of San Juan Hill during the Spanish-American War [1898] was named "Texas."

In 1901, President Theodore Roosevelt [1901-09] officially established the "White House" name by having executive letterheads printed to read:

White House—Washington

When Franklin Delano Roosevelt (1882 – 1945) entered the "White House" in 1933 he did his fifth cousin one better by adding "The" and commissioning the engraving in a new arrangement:

The White House
Washington

First constructed in 1792, the building was variously called the "President's Palace," the "President's House" and the most often used "Executive Mansion." Since 1811, however, it was jokingly referred to as the "White House."

President Theodore Roosevelt [1901-09]wore a ring containing a lock of Abraham Lincoln's hair at his inauguration of March 4, 1905.

The hair had been cut by one of Lincoln's attending physicians following the assassination, Dr. Charles Sabin Taft (1835 – 1900), to access the fatal wound.

William Howard Taft (1857 – 1930), who weighed 325 lbs during his presidency [1909-13], had a bathtub installed in the White House large enough to hold four men.

President Woodrow Wilson's [1913-21] portrait appears on the $100,000 bill [Series 1934, Gold Certificate]. Although out of print, it is still considered legal tender.

Courtesy:
United States Department of Treasury
1500 Pennsylvania Avenue NW
Washington, DC 20220
[Note: Fraudulent enlargement and/or use of this
image is punishable under present counterfeiting laws.]

The *Rutherford B. Hayes Center Presidential Library* Spiegel Grove, Fremont, Ohio was the first presidential library established. It was dedicated on May 30, 1916.

A western enthusiast, President Calvin Coolidge [1923-29] had a mechanical horse installed in his White House bedroom, where he rode it nearly every day.

Herbert Hoover's (1874 – 1964) 1932 presidential campaign slogan, "A chicken in every pot," originated with France's King Henry IV (1553 – 1610) who, at his coronation on February 27, 1574, said it was his hope "to make France so prosperous every peasant will have a chicken in his pot on Sunday."

President Franklin Delano Roosevelt [1933-45] appeared as himself in *Princess O'Rourke*, the 1943 romantic comedy movie starring Olivia de Haviland in the title role.

President Harry S. Truman [1945-53] had only a middle initial, not a middle name. The explanation for this has always been ambiguous, even from Truman himself.

Dwight David Eisenhower (1890 – 1969) was the first President of the United States [1953-61] born in Texas.

Samuel James Seymoure (ca 1860 – 1956), watching *Our American Cousin* at Ford's Theater with his godmother, Mrs. George S. Goldsborough, was the last surviving witness to President Abraham Lincoln's assassination of 1865. He died ninety-one years to the day of the tragic event [April 14, 1956].

Ronald Reagan (1911–2004) was the only United States President [1981-89] born in Illinois, "The Land of Lincoln." [Note: Abraham Lincoln (1809 – 1865) was actually born at Sinking Spring Farm, southeast Hardin County, Kentucky.]

On October 11, 2002, Jimmy Carter won the Alfred Nobel Peace Prize, making him the third United States President [1977-81] to win the honor after Theodore Roosevelt [1906] and Woodrow Wilson [1919].

On October 17, 2002, former President William J. Clinton [1993-2001] became an honorary inductee into the Arkansas Black Hall of Fame, making him the first white person recognized by the hall.

"In wilderness I sense the miracle of life, and behind it
our scientific accomplishments fade to trivia."
Charles A. Lindbergh
(1902 – 1974)
American aviator

World Trivia

Did You Know:

Argentina, South America was home to the early human Patagonian giants in the 8th millennium B.C.E.

Socrates (469 – 399 B.C.E.), the famous Greek philosopher, once said: "Children today are tyrants. They contradict their parents, gobble their food and tyrannize their teachers."

The windmill originated in Persia [modern Iran], to grind grain, in 644 B.C.E.

The world's oldest active brewery, dating back to 1040 C.E., is in Weihenstephan, Germany.

Belgian mechanic John Joseph Merlin (1735 – 1803) demonstrated the roller skate [his invention] for the first time at a London masquerade party [1760].

Mount Everest is named for Sir George Everest (1790 – 1866), who led The Great Trigonometrical Survey of India from 1823 to 1830. [Appointed Surveyor-General of India, 1830-43.]

Sir George Everest
(1790 – 1866)
British surveyor
Photo in author's collection

Queen Victoria (1819 – 1901)was 18-years-old when she

attained command of the United Kingdom of Great Britain and Ireland in 1837. She would reign for sixty-three years, seven months [1837-1901], making her the longest sitting English monarch to date.

Unjustly convicted by the French military as a "double agent" during World War I, exotic dancer Marta Hari was born in Friesland, Netherlands as Magaretha Geertruida Zelle (1876 – 1917).

She was executed by firing squad on October 15, 1917 and, although erroneous, her legend as a notorious female enemy agent lives on.

Marta Hari in 1915
(1876 – 1917)
Unjustly convicted and executed as a
"double agent" during World War I.
Photo in author's collection
[Photographer unknown]

When he opened a chain of 5-and-10-cent stores in England [1909], F.W. Woolworth (1852 – 1919) called them "Three-and-sixpence" stores.

London's famous Big Ben is not the Clock Tower, but the bell housed within the Clock Tower of the House of Parliament, in the Palace of Winchester.

Radio City Music Hall, New York City [opened December 27, 1932], is the largest active movie theater in the United States today.

Switzerland, neutral since 1815 and one of the founding members of the *League of Nations* [1919-46] did not join the *United Nations* until September 10, 2002.

"Don't worry about the world coming to an end today. It's already tomorrow in Australia."
Charles Monroe Shultz
(1922 – 2000)
American cartoonist
Creator of: *Peanuts*

"The art and science of ask-ing questions is the source of all knowledge."

Thomas Berger
American novelist
Author of: *Little Big Man*

Index of Subjects

A

Abomination, 46
Academy of Ancient Arts, 33
Adam, 104
Adams, John, 23, 107, 128
Adrian IV, Pope, 42
A Farewell to Arms, 39
African-American, 36-37
Alabama, 67
Alaska, 131
Alaska, Juneau, 27
Alexandria, Lighthouse of, 53
Allegheny Aqueduct Bridge, 108
All Star Comics #8, 49
Amazons, 49
America, 28, 50, 65, 67, 69, 105, 109
American, 21, 23, 26, 30, 34, 49, 60, 75, 96, 100, 109, 116
American Gothic, 38
Amyitis, 54
Analytical Engine, 115

Index

Index

Index

C

Index

Index

D

Index

Index

Index

Index

H

Index

Index

Index

Index

Index

M

Index

Index

Index

Index

Index

Index

Index

Index

Index

Index

X

Index

Y
Young, Brigham, 98
You're a Good Man, Charlie Brown, 124
Youth's Companion [magazine], 28

Z
Zeus [Greek king of the gods], 104
Zimmerman Telegram, 80
Zorro [Mexican legendary hero], 48

"As a single footstep will not make a path on earth, so a single thought will not make a pathway to the mind.

"To make a deep physical path, we walk again and again.

"To make a deep mental path, we must think over and over the kind of thoughts we wish to dominate our lives."

Henry David Thoreau

(1817 – 1862)

American writer, naturalist, philosopher

About the Author

Dr. Bouffard holds an LL.B. from LaSalle University, a Masters and Psy.D. from Neotarian College of Psychology. And has applied thirty years to psychological counseling.

In 1999, he earned a Ph.D. (a candidacy shelved for twenty years due to time restraints) in Theocentric Business and Ethics from American College of Metaphysical Theology, leading to ministerial credentials.

His lifelong fascination with history has led him to currently author several papers and books in this genre.